I would like to dedicate this book to Eddie Carey Chisholm Sr.,
my lovable Dad who always encouraged me to pursue my talent in writing.
Also to my loving husband Willie Chavers,
and daughters Whitney and Kelli Chavers…
Thank you for supporting my dreams.

Love,

Kathy

Published by Chavers Publishing

2008 Kathy Chisholm Chavers

Written By Kathy Chisholm Chavers

Illustrator Paul Edwards III

Editing by Lilmissdottie: The Word Stylist

Arranged by Aspects Publishing and Accent Your Vibe

kmariac@sbcglobal.net

Printed in the United States of America
2008

ISBN 978-1-60585-530-1

Stinky Winky was always stinky.

Stinky Winky never had any friends. He played with his toys all day if he pleased.

Stinky Winky liked to play in the trash, jump in the mud puddles and never thought about a bath.

Stinky ate all kinds of germy foods. He never worried about how dirty it was. He just ate and ate till he could eat no more.

His Mom would say “Stinky, please come take a bath.” But Stinky would look at Mom and say “No Mom, I don’t want to take a bath.” I like how I am.”

Dad tried to catch Stinky to take a nice bath, but Stinky would out run his Dad, running very, very fast.

Mom and Dad thought long and hard. "We have to get this boy a bath!"

With lots of thinking, they had a great plan!

"Winky we have a super game we know you will like."
"We will play Pirates and you can be the first to walk the plank."

Mom and Dad took Winky's swimming pool, filled it with nice soapy water and covered the top of the pool. Winky would never know it was a trap.

Stinky said, “ Oh wow, this will be fun!”

With speed Stinky jumped off the plank into the water only to land in clean soapy water! (Plop!)

“Mom, Dad, what did you do?”
“Well, Winky we wanted a clean little boy.”

When the bath was over and Winky was dressed,
Winky looked in the mirror and saw something great!

Never again will he be called Stinky Winky but Mom and Dad's loveable WINKY!